VIOLIN

101 HIT SONGS

Available for
FLUTE, CLARINET, ALTO SAX, TENOR SAX, TRUMPET,
HORN, TROMBONE, VIOLIN, VIOLA, CELLO

ISBN 978-1-4950-7535-3

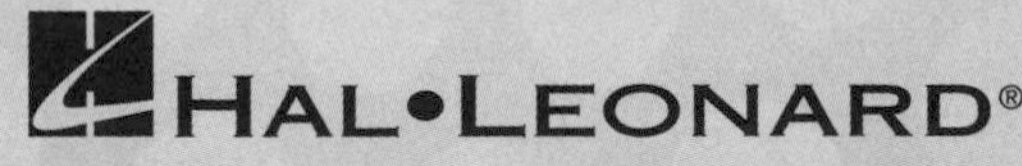

7777 W. Bluemound Rd. P.O. Box 13819 Milwaukee, WI 53213

Visit Hal Leonard Online at
www.halleonard.com

CONTENTS

ALL ABOUT THAT BASS

VIOLIN

Words and Music by KEVIN KADISH
and MEGHAN TRAINOR

AMAZED

VIOLIN

Words and Music by MARV GREEN,
CHRIS LINDSEY and AIMEE MAYO

ALL OF ME

VIOLIN

Words and Music by JOHN STEPHENS
and TOBY GAD

1.
1st time D.C.
2nd Time Fine
2.
D.S. al Fine
(take 1st ending)

APOLOGIZE

VIOLIN

Words and Music by
RYAN TEDDER

BEAUTIFUL

VIOLIN

Words and Music by
LINDA PERRY

BAD DAY

VIOLIN

Words and Music by
DANIEL POWTER

D.S. al Coda
CODA

BAD ROMANCE

VIOLIN

Words and Music by STEFANI GERMANOTTA
and NADIR KHAYAT

BEAUTIFUL DAY

VIOLIN

Words by BONO
Music by U2

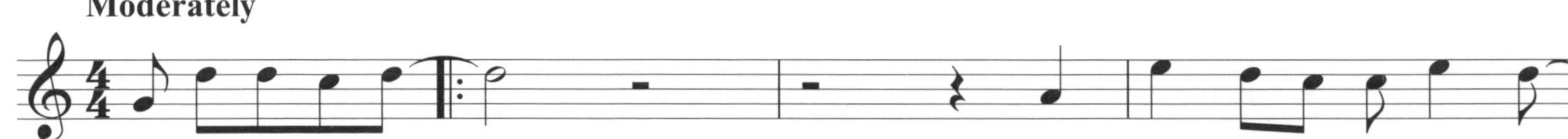

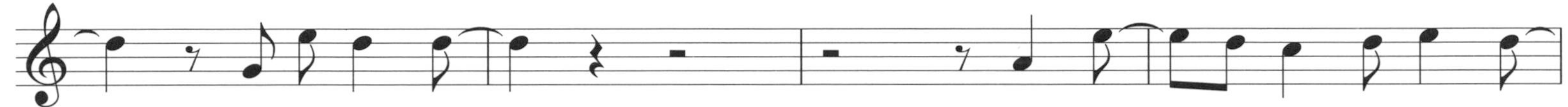

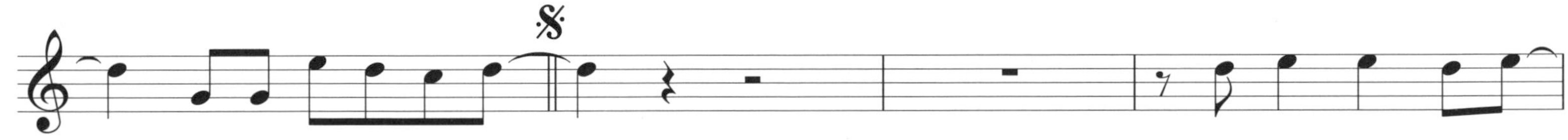

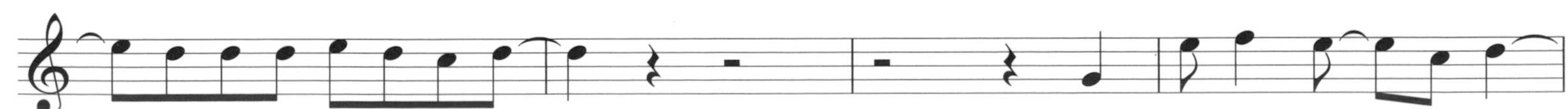

To Coda
1.
3
2.
D.S. al Coda
CODA

BEAUTIFUL IN MY EYES

VIOLIN

Words and Music by
JOSHUA KADISON

BECAUSE I LOVE YOU
(The Postman Song)

VIOLIN

Words and Music by
WARREN BROOKS

BELIEVE

VIOLIN

Words and Music by BRIAN HIGGINS,
STUART McLENNEN, PAUL BARRY,
STEPHEN TORCH, MATT GRAY
and TIM POWELL

BUTTERFLY KISSES

VIOLIN

Words and Music by BOB CARLISLE
and RANDY THOMAS

BRAVE

VIOLIN

Words and Music by SARA BAREILLES
and JACK ANTONOFF

To Coda
D.S. al Coda
CODA

BREAKAWAY

from THE PRINCESS DIARIES 2: ROYAL ENGAGEMENT

VIOLIN

Words and Music by BRIDGET BENENATE, AVRIL LAVIGNE and MATTHEW GERRARD

BREATHE

VIOLIN

Words and Music by HOLLY LAMAR
and STEPHANIE BENTLEY

To Coda
1.
2.
D.S. al Coda
CODA
2

CALL ME MAYBE

VIOLIN

Words and Music by CARLY RAE JEPSEN,
JOSHUA RAMSAY and TAVISH CROWE

To Coda
D.S. al Coda
(no repeat)
CODA

CANDLE IN THE WIND 1997

VIOLIN

Words and Music by ELTON JOHN
and BERNIE TAUPIN

CHANGE THE WORLD

featured on the Motion Picture Soundtrack PHENOMENON

VIOLIN

Words and Music by WAYNE KIRKPATRICK,
GORDON KENNEDY and TOMMY SIMS

CHASING CARS

VIOLIN

Words and Music by GARY LIGHTBODY,
TOM SIMPSON, PAUL WILSON,
JONATHAN QUINN and NATHAN CONNOLLY

THE CLIMB

from HANNAH MONTANA: THE MOVIE

VIOLIN

Words and Music by JESSI ALEXANDER and JON MABE

CLOCKS

VIOLIN

Words and Music by GUY BERRYMAN,
JON BUCKLAND, WILL CHAMPION
and CHRIS MARTIN

DON'T KNOW WHY

VIOLIN

Words and Music by
JESSE HARRIS

COUNTDOWN

VIOLIN

Words and Music by BEYONCÉ KNOWLES,
CAINON LAMB, JULIE FROST, MICHAEL BIVINS,
ESTHER DEAN, TERIUS NASH, SHEA TAYLOR,
NATHAN MORRIS and WANYA MORRIS

- contains sample of "Uhh Ahh"

2nd time, D.C. al Coda
CODA

CRUISE

VIOLIN

Words and Music by CHASE RICE,
TYLER HUBBARD, BRIAN KELLEY,
JOEY MOI and JESSE RICE

Moderately, in 2

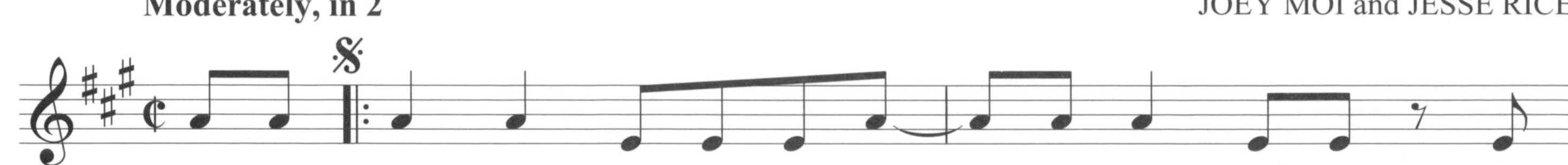

To Coda
1.
2.
D.S. al Coda
CODA
3

CRYIN'

VIOLIN

Words and Music by STEVEN TYLER,
JOE PERRY and TAYLOR RHODES

Fine
1.
2.
D.S. al Fine

DIE A HAPPY MAN

VIOLIN

Words and Music by THOMAS RHETT,
JOE SPARGUR and SEAN DOUGLAS

1.
2.

DILEMMA

VIOLIN

Words and Music by CORNELL HAYNES,
ANTWON MAKER, KENNETH GAMBLE
and BUNNY SIGLER

Fine
2nd time, D.S. al Fine

DRIFT AWAY

VIOLIN

Words and Music by
MENTOR WILLIAMS

FIELDS OF GOLD

VIOLIN

Music and Lyrics by
STING

DROPS OF JUPITER
(Tell Me)

VIOLIN

Words and Music by PAT MONAHAN,
JAMES STAFFORD, ROBERT HOTCHKISS,
CHARLES COLIN and SCOTT UNDERWOOD

D.S. al Coda
CODA

FALLIN'

VIOLIN

Words and Music by
ALICIA KEYS

1., 2.
3.

FIREWORK

VIOLIN

Words and Music by KATY PERRY,
MIKKEL ERIKSEN, TOR ERIK HERMANSEN,
ESTHER DEAN and SANDY WILHELM

To Coda
D.S. al Coda
CODA

FOOLISH GAMES

VIOLIN

Words and Music by
JEWEL KILCHER

3
3
3
3

FOREVER AND FOR ALWAYS

VIOLIN

Words and Music by SHANIA TWAIN
and R.J. LANGE

1.
2.

FRIENDS IN LOW PLACES

VIOLIN

Words and Music by DeWAYNE BLACKWELL
and EARL BUD LEE

FROM A DISTANCE

VIOLIN

Words and Music by
JULIE GOLD

Moderately slow

To Coda

1. 2.

D.S. al Coda

CODA

GENIE IN A BOTTLE

VIOLIN

Words and Music by STEVE KIPNER,
DAVID FRANK and PAMELA SHEYNE

1.
3
2.
To Coda
2nd time, D.S. al Coda
(take 2nd ending)
CODA

GET LUCKY

VIOLIN

Words and Music by THOMAS BANGALTER,
GUY MANUEL HOMEM CHRISTO, NILE RODGERS
and PHARRELL WILLIAMS

HOW TO SAVE A LIFE

VIOLIN

Words and Music by JOSEPH KING
and ISAAC SLADE

HELLO

VIOLIN

Words and Music by ADELE ADKINS
and GREG KURSTIN

1.
2.

HERE AND NOW

VIOLIN

Words and Music by TERRY STEELE
and DAVID ELLIOT

To Coda
1.
2.
D.S. al Coda
CODA

HERO

VIOLIN

Words and Music by ENRIQUE IGLESIAS,
PAUL BARRY and MARK TAYLOR

1.
2.
1., 2.
3.

HEY, SOUL SISTER

VIOLIN

Words and Music by PAT MONAHAN,
ESPEN LIND and AMUND BJORKLUND

To Coda
1.
2.
D.S. al Coda
CODA
1.
2.

HO HEY

VIOLIN

Words and Music by JEREMY FRAITES
and WESLEY SCHULTZ

Moderately slow, in 2

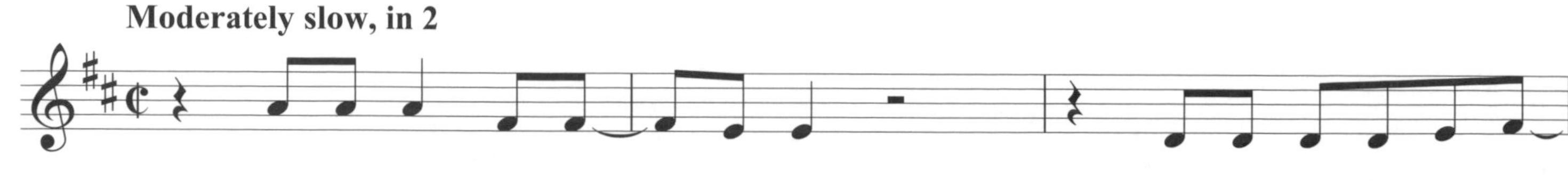

1.
Fine
2.
D.S. al Fine
(take 1st ending)

HOLD ON, WE'RE GOING HOME

VIOLIN

Words and Music by AUBREY GRAHAM,
PAUL JEFFERIES, NOAH SHEBIB,
JORDAN ULLMAN and MAJID AL-MASKATI

Moderately

1.
Fine
2.
1.
2.
D.S. al Fine
(take 1st ending)

HOME

VIOLIN

Words and Music by GREG HOLDEN
and DREW PEARSON

THE HOUSE THAT BUILT ME

VIOLIN

Words and Music by TOM DOUGLAS
and ALLEN SHAMBLIN

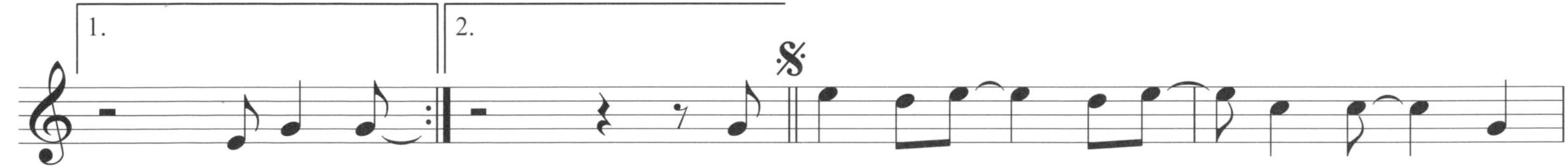

Fine
D.S. al Fine

HOW AM I SUPPOSED TO LIVE WITHOUT YOU

VIOLIN

Words and Music by MICHAEL BOLTON
and DOUG JAMES

1.
2.

I FINALLY FOUND SOMEONE

from THE MIRROR HAS TWO FACES

VIOLIN

Words and Music by BARBRA STREISAND,
MARVIN HAMLISCH, R.J. LANGE
and BRYAN ADAMS

Fine
D.S. al Fine

I GOTTA FEELING

VIOLIN

Words and Music by WILL ADAMS,
ALLAN PINEDA, JAIME GOMEZ, STACY FERGUSON,
DAVID GUETTA and FREDERIC RIESTERER

1.
2.
To Coda
D.S. al Coda
(take repeat)
CODA

I KISSED A GIRL

VIOLIN

Words and Music by KATY PERRY,
CATHY DENNIS, MAX MARTIN
and LUKASZ GOTTWALD

1.
Fine
2.
D.S. al Fine
(take 1st ending)

I SWEAR

VIOLIN

Words and Music by FRANK MYERS
and GARY BAKER

I WILL REMEMBER YOU

Theme from THE BROTHERS McMULLEN

VIOLIN

Words and Music by SARAH McLACHLAN,
SEAMUS EGAN and DAVE MERENDA

JAR OF HEARTS

VIOLIN

Words and Music by BARRETT YERETSIAN,
CHRISTINA PERRI and DREW LAWRENCE

D.S. al Coda
CODA
3
3

JUST THE WAY YOU ARE

VIOLIN

Words and Music by BRUNO MARS,
ARI LEVINE, PHILIP LAWRENCE,
KHARI CAIN and KHALIL WALTON

To Coda
Fine
D.S. al Coda
CODA
D.S. al Fine

LIPS OF AN ANGEL

VIOLIN

Words and Music by AUSTIN WINKLER,
ROSS HANSON, LLOYD GARVEY, MARK KING,
MICHAEL RODDEN and BRIAN HOWES

Slowly

1.
2.

LITTLE TALKS

VIOLIN

Words and Music by
OF MONSTERS AND MEN

1.
2.

LET IT GO

VIOLIN

Words and Music by JAMES BAY
and PAUL BARRY

NEED YOU NOW

VIOLIN

Words and Music by HILLARY SCOTT,
CHARLES KELLEY, DAVE HAYWOOD
and JOSH KEAR

LOSING MY RELIGION

VIOLIN

Words and Music by WILLIAM BERRY,
PETER BUCK, MICHAEL MILLS
and MICHAEL STIPE

Moderately fast

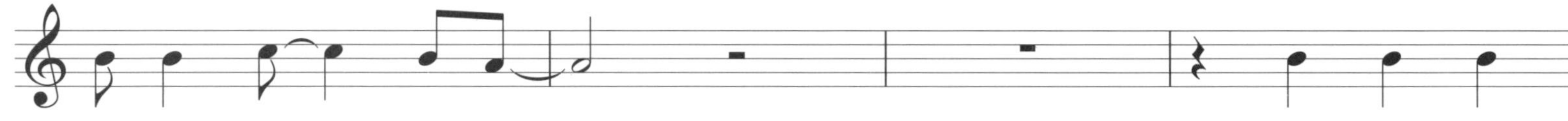

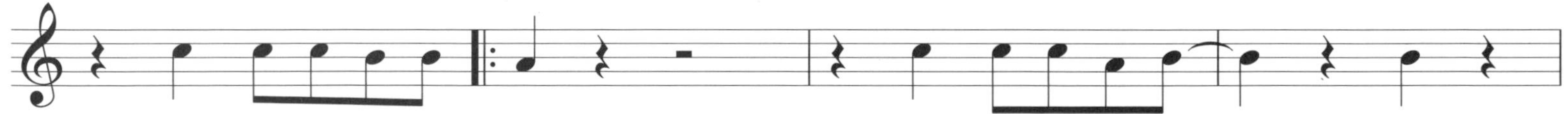

1.
2.

LOVE SONG

VIOLIN

Words and Music by
SARA BAREILLES

Fine
D.S. al Fine

LOVE STORY

VIOLIN

Words and Music by
TAYLOR SWIFT

Moderately

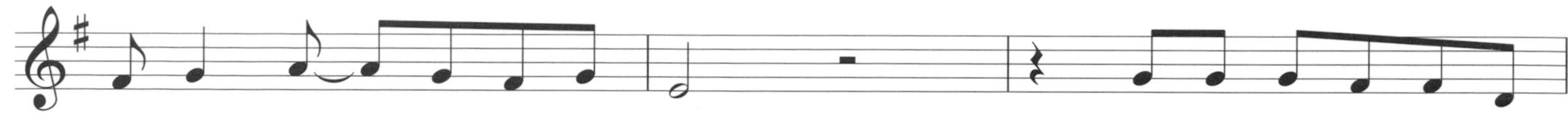

To Coda
1.
2.
D.S al Coda
CODA

MORE THAN WORDS

VIOLIN

Words and Music by NUNO BETTENCOURT
and GARY CHERONE

1.
2.

NO ONE

VIOLIN

Words and Music by ALICIA KEYS,
KERRY BROTHERS, JR. and GEORGE HARRY

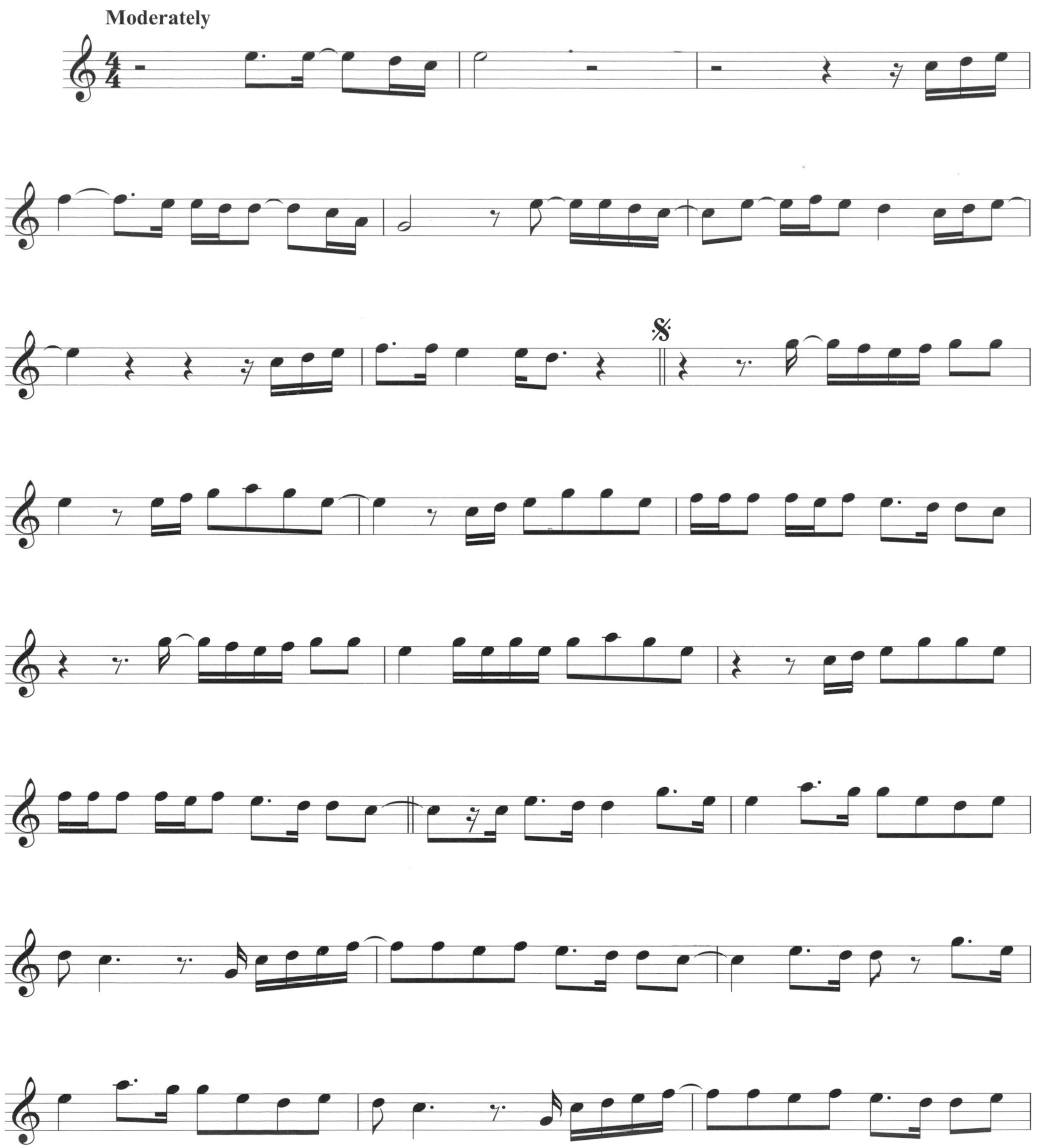

To Coda
D.S. al Coda
CODA

100 YEARS

VIOLIN

Words and Music by
JOHN ONDRASIK

Moderately fast

To Coda

1.

D.C.
(with repeat)

2.

D.C al Coda
(no repeat)

CODA

REHAB

VIOLIN

Words and Music by
AMY WINEHOUSE

THE POWER OF LOVE

VIOLIN

Words by MARY SUSAN APPLEGATE
and JENNIFER RUSH
Music by CANDY DEROUGE
and GUNTHER MENDE

1.
2.
Fine
D.S. al Fine
(take 2nd ending)

ROAR

VIOLIN

Words and Music by KATY PERRY,
LUKASZ GOTTWALD, MAX MARTIN,
BONNIE McKEE and HENRY WALTER

ROLLING IN THE DEEP

VIOLIN

Words and Music by ADELE ADKINS
and PAUL EPWORTH

ROYALS

VIOLIN

Words and Music by ELLA YELICH-O'CONNOR
and JOEL LITTLE

SAVE THE BEST FOR LAST

VIOLIN

Words and Music by WENDY WALDMAN,
PHIL GALDSTON and JON LIND

SAY SOMETHING

VIOLIN

Words and Music by IAN AXEL,
CHAD VACCARINO and MIKE CAMPBELL

SHAKE IT OFF

VIOLIN

Words and Music by TAYLOR SWIFT,
MAX MARTIN and SHELLBACK

SECRETS

VIOLIN

Words and Music by
RYAN TEDDER

2nd time, to Coda
3rd time, Fine
D.S. al Coda
CODA
D.S. al Fine

SHE WILL BE LOVED

VIOLIN

Words and Music by ADAM LEVINE
and JAMES VALENTINE

SMELLS LIKE TEEN SPIRIT

VIOLIN

Words and Music by KURT COBAIN,
KRIST NOVOSELIC and DAVE GROHL

SOMETHING TO TALK ABOUT
(Let's Give Them Something to Talk About)

VIOLIN

Words and Music by
SHIRLEY EIKHARD

STAY WITH ME

VIOLIN

Words and Music by SAM SMITH,
JAMES NAPIER, WILLIAM EDWARD PHILLIPS,
TOM PETTY and JEFF LYNNE

STACY'S MOM

VIOLIN

Words and Music by CHRIS COLLINGWOOD
and ADAM SCHLESINGER

STAY

VIOLIN

Words and Music by MIKKY EKKO
and JUSTIN PARKER

Moderately

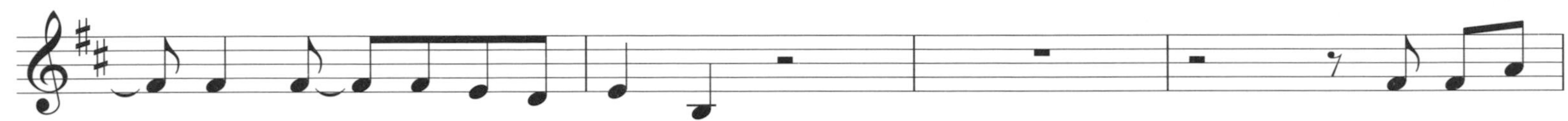

Fine
3
D.S. al Fine

STRONGER
(What Doesn't Kill You)

VIOLIN

Words and Music by GREG KURSTIN,
JORGEN ELOFSSON, DAVID GAMSON
and ALEXANDRA TAMPOSI

2nd time, to Coda
3rd time, Fine
D.S. al Coda
CODA
D.S. al Fine

TEARS IN HEAVEN

VIOLIN

Words and Music by ERIC CLAPTON
and WILL JENNINGS

TEENAGE DREAM

VIOLIN

Words and Music by KATY PERRY,
BONNIE McKEE, LUKASZ GOTTWALD,
MAX MARTIN and BENJAMIN LEVIN

THINKING OUT LOUD

VIOLIN

Words and Music by ED SHEERAN
and AMY WADGE

1.
2.

THIS LOVE

VIOLIN

Words and Music by ADAM LEVINE
and JESSE CARMICHAEL

A THOUSAND YEARS

from the Summit Entertainment film THE TWILIGHT SAGE: BREAKING DAWN - PART 1

VIOLIN

Words and Music by DAVID HODGES
and CHRISTINA PERRI

TILL THE WORLD ENDS

VIOLIN

Words and Music by LUKASZ GOTTWALD,
MAX MARTIN, KESHA SEBERT
and ALEXANDER KRONLUND

Moderately fast

4th time, to Coda
1.
2.
D.C. al Coda
(take repeat)
CODA

UPTOWN FUNK

VIOLIN

Words and Music by MARK RONSON,
BRUNO MARS, PHILIP LAWRENCE, JEFF BHASKER, DEVON GALLASPY,
NICHOLAUS WILLIAMS, LONNIE SIMMONS, RONNIE WILSON,
CHARLES WILSON, RUDOLPH TAYLOR and ROBERT WILSON

1.
2.
To Coda
D.S. al Coda
(take repeat)
CODA

VIVA LA VIDA

VIOLIN

Words and Music by GUY BERRYMAN,
JON BUCKLAND, WILL CHAMPION
and CHRIS MARTIN

Moderately

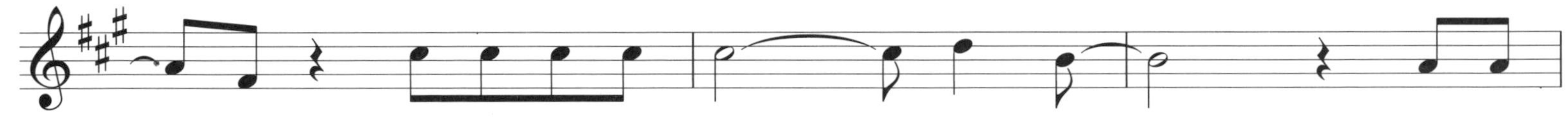

WAITING ON THE WORLD TO CHANGE

VIOLIN

Words and Music by
JOHN MAYER

WE CAN'T STOP

VIOLIN

Words and Music by MILEY CYRUS,
THERON THOMAS, TIMOTHY THOMAS, MICHAEL WILLIAMS,
PIERRE SLAUGHTER, DOUGLAS DAVIS and RICKY WALTERS

WE BELONG TOGETHER

VIOLIN

Words and Music by MARIAH CAREY,
JERMAINE DUPRI, MANUEL SEAL, JOHNTA AUSTIN,
DARNELL BRISTOL, KENNETH EDMONDS, SIDNEY JOHNSON,
PATRICK MOTEN, BOBBY WOMACK and SANDRA SULLY

To Coda
D.S. al Coda
CODA

WE FOUND LOVE

VIOLIN

Words and Music by
CALVIN HARRIS

WHAT MAKES YOU BEAUTIFUL

VIOLIN

Words and Music by SAVAN KOTECHA,
RAMI YACOUB and CARL FALK

WHEN YOU SAY NOTHING AT ALL

VIOLIN

Words and Music by DON SCHLITZ
and PAUL OVERSTREET

YOU RAISE ME UP

VIOLIN

Words and Music by BRENDAN GRAHAM
and ROLF LOVLAND

YEAH!

VIOLIN

Words and Music by JAMES PHILLIPS,
LA MARQUIS JEFFERSON, CHRISTOPHER BRIDGES,
JONATHAN SMITH and SEAN GARRETT

1.
2.
Fine
D.S. al Fine
(take repeat)

YOU WERE MEANT FOR ME

VIOLIN

Words and Music by JEWEL MURRAY
and STEVE POLTZ

To Coda
1.
2.
3
Slowly, freely
D.C. al Coda
CODA

YOU'RE BEAUTIFUL

VIOLIN

Words and Music by JAMES BLUNT,
SACHA SKARBEK and AMANDA GHOST

YOU'RE STILL THE ONE

VIOLIN

Words and Music by SHANIA TWAIN
and R.J. LANGE

YOU'VE GOT A FRIEND IN ME

from Walt Disney's TOY STORY

VIOLIN

Music and Lyrics by
RANDY NEWMAN

101 SONGS

BIG COLLECTIONS OF FAVORITE SONGS
ARRANGED FOR SOLO INSTRUMENTALISTS.

101 BROADWAY SONGS

00154199	Flute	$15.99
00154200	Clarinet	$15.99
00154201	Alto Sax	$15.99
00154202	Tenor Sax	$16.99
00154203	Trumpet	$15.99
00154204	Horn	$15.99
00154205	Trombone	$15.99
00154206	Violin	$15.99
00154207	Viola	$15.99
00154208	Cello	$15.99

101 DISNEY SONGS

00244104	Flute	$17.99
00244106	Clarinet	$17.99
00244107	Alto Sax	$17.99
00244108	Tenor Sax	$17.99
00244109	Trumpet	$17.99
00244112	Horn	$17.99
00244120	Trombone	$17.99
00244121	Violin	$17.99
00244125	Viola	$17.99
00244126	Cello	$17.99

101 MOVIE HITS

00158087	Flute	$15.99
00158088	Clarinet	$15.99
00158089	Alto Sax	$15.99
00158090	Tenor Sax	$15.99
00158091	Trumpet	$15.99
00158092	Horn	$15.99
00158093	Trombone	$15.99
00158094	Violin	$15.99
00158095	Viola	$15.99
00158096	Cello	$15.99

101 CHRISTMAS SONGS

00278637	Flute	$15.99
00278638	Clarinet	$15.99
00278639	Alto Sax	$15.99
00278640	Tenor Sax	$15.99
00278641	Trumpet	$15.99
00278642	Horn	$14.99
00278643	Trombone	$15.99
00278644	Violin	$15.99
00278645	Viola	$15.99
00278646	Cello	$15.99

101 HIT SONGS

00194561	Flute	$17.99
00197182	Clarinet	$17.99
00197183	Alto Sax	$17.99
00197184	Tenor Sax	$17.99
00197185	Trumpet	$17.99
00197186	Horn	$17.99
00197187	Trombone	$17.99
00197188	Violin	$17.99
00197189	Viola	$17.99
00197190	Cello	$17.99

101 POPULAR SONGS

00224722	Flute	$17.99
00224723	Clarinet	$17.99
00224724	Alto Sax	$17.99
00224725	Tenor Sax	$17.99
00224726	Trumpet	$17.99
00224727	Horn	$17.99
00224728	Trombone	$17.99
00224729	Violin	$17.99
00224730	Viola	$17.99
00224731	Cello	$17.99

101 CLASSICAL THEMES

00155315	Flute	$15.99
00155317	Clarinet	$15.99
00155318	Alto Sax	$15.99
00155319	Tenor Sax	$15.99
00155320	Trumpet	$15.99
00155321	Horn	$15.99
00155322	Trombone	$15.99
00155323	Violin	$15.99
00155324	Viola	$15.99
00155325	Cello	$15.99

101 JAZZ SONGS

00146363	Flute	$15.99
00146364	Clarinet	$15.99
00146366	Alto Sax	$15.99
00146367	Tenor Sax	$15.99
00146368	Trumpet	$15.99
00146369	Horn	$14.99
00146370	Trombone	$15.99
00146371	Violin	$15.99
00146372	Viola	$15.99
00146373	Cello	$15.99

101 MOST BEAUTIFUL SONGS

00291023	Flute	$16.99
00291041	Clarinet	$16.99
00291042	Alto Sax	$17.99
00291043	Tenor Sax	$17.99
00291044	Trumpet	$16.99
00291045	Horn	$16.99
00291046	Trombone	$16.99
00291047	Violin	$16.99
00291048	Viola	$16.99
00291049	Cello	$17.99

See complete song lists and sample pages at www.halleonard.com

Prices, contents and availability subject to change without notice.

101 TIPS FROM HAL LEONARD

STUFF ALL THE PROS KNOW AND USE

Ready to take your skills to the next level? These books present valuable how-to insight that musicians of all styles and levels can benefit from. The text, photos, music, diagrams and accompanying audio provide a terrific, easy-to-use resource for a variety of topics.

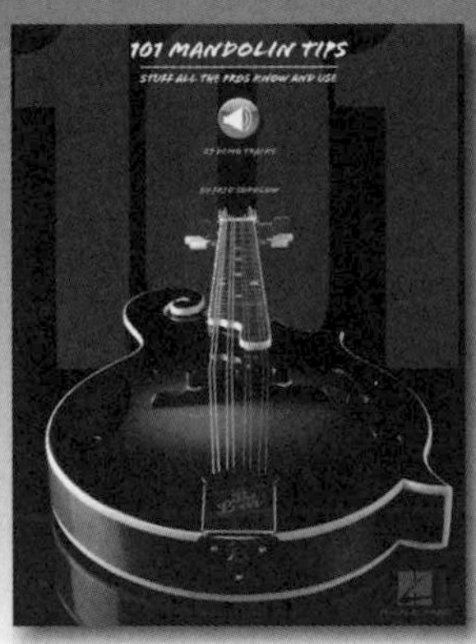

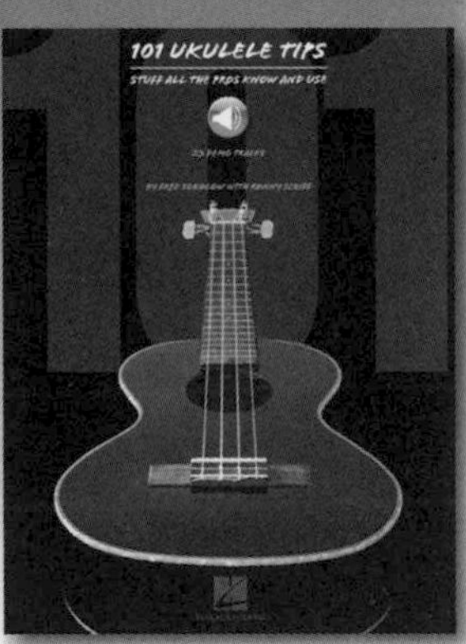

101 HAMMOND B-3 TIPS
by Brian Charette
Topics include: funky scales and modes; unconventional harmonies; creative chord voicings; cool drawbar settings; ear-grabbing special effects; professional gigging advice; practicing effectively; making good use of the pedals; and much more!
00128918 Book/Online Audio $14.99

101 HARMONICA TIPS
by Steve Cohen
Topics include: techniques, position playing, soloing, accompaniment, the blues, equipment, performance, maintenance, and much more!
00821040 Book/Online Audio $17.99

101 CELLO TIPS—2ND EDITION
by Angela Schmidt
Topics include: bowing techniques, non-classical playing, electric cellos, accessories, gig tips, practicing, recording and much more!
00149094 Book/Online Audio $14.99

101 FLUTE TIPS
by Elaine Schmidt
Topics include: selecting the right flute for you, finding the right teacher, warm-up exercises, practicing effectively, taking good care of your flute, gigging advice, staying and playing healthy, and much more.
00119883 Book/CD Pack.................................$14.99

101 SAXOPHONE TIPS
by Eric Morones
Topics include: techniques; maintenance; equipment; practicing; recording; performance; and much more!
00311082 Book/CD Pack.................................$19.99

101 TRUMPET TIPS
by Scott Barnard
Topics include: techniques, articulation, tone production, soloing, exercises, special effects, equipment, performance, maintenance and much more.
00312082 Book/CD Pack.................................$14.99

101 UPRIGHT BASS TIPS
by Andy McKee
Topics include: right- and left-hand technique, improvising and soloing, practicing, proper care of the instrument, ear training, performance, and much more.
00102009 Book/Online Audio $14.99

101 BASS TIPS
by Gary Willis
Topics include: techniques, improvising and soloing, equipment, practicing, ear training, performance, theory, and much more.
00695542 Book/Online Audio $19.99

101 DRUM TIPS—2ND EDITION
Topics include: grooves, practicing, warming up, tuning, gear, performance, and much more!
00151936 Book/Online Audio $14.99

101 FIVE-STRING BANJO TIPS
by Fred Sokolow
Topics include: techniques, ear training, performance, and much more!
00696647 Book/CD Pack.................................$14.99

101 GUITAR TIPS
by Adam St. James
Topics include: scales, music theory, truss rod adjustments, proper recording studio set-ups, and much more. The book also features snippets of advice from some of the most celebrated guitarists and producers in the music business.
00695737 Book/Online Audio $17.99

101 MANDOLIN TIPS
by Fred Sokolow
Topics include: playing tips, practicing tips, accessories, mandolin history and lore, practical music theory, and much more!
00119493 Book/Online Audio $14.99

101 RECORDING TIPS
by Adam St. James
This book contains recording tips, suggestions, and advice learned firsthand from legendary producers, engineers, and artists. These tricks of the trade will improve anyone's home or pro studio recordings.
00311035 Book/CD Pack.................................$14.95

101 UKULELE TIPS
by Fred Sokolow with Ronny Schiff
Topics include: techniques, improvising and soloing, equipment, practicing, ear training, performance, uke history and lore, and much more!
00696596 Book/Online Audio $15.99

101 VIOLIN TIPS
by Angela Schmidt
Topics include: bowing techniques, non-classical playing, electric violins, accessories, gig tips, practicing, recording, and much more!
00842672 Book/CD Pack.................................$14.99

Prices, contents and availability subject to change without notice.

www.halleonard.com

HAL•LEONARD INSTRUMENTAL PLAY-ALONG

Your favorite songs are arranged just for solo instrumentalists with this outstanding series. Each book includes great full-accompaniment play-along audio so you can sound just like a pro!

Check out **halleonard.com** for songlists and more titles!

12 Pop Hits
12 songs
00261790 Flute · 00261795 Horn
00261791 Clarinet · 00261796 Trombone
00261792 Alto Sax · 00261797 Violin
00261793 Tenor Sax · 00261798 Viola
00261794 Trumpet · 00261799 Cello

The Very Best of Bach
15 selections
00225371 Flute · 00225376 Horn
00225372 Clarinet · 00225377 Trombone
00225373 Alto Sax · 00225378 Violin
00225374 Tenor Sax · 00225379 Viola
00225375 Trumpet · 00225380 Cello

The Beatles
15 songs
00225330 Flute · 00225335 Horn
00225331 Clarinet · 00225336 Trombone
00225332 Alto Sax · 00225337 Violin
00225333 Tenor Sax · 00225338 Viola
00225334 Trumpet · 00225339 Cello

Chart Hits
12 songs
00146207 Flute · 00146212 Horn
00146208 Clarinet · 00146213 Trombone
00146209 Alto Sax · 00146214 Violin
00146210 Tenor Sax · 00146211 Trumpet
00146216 Cello

Christmas Songs
12 songs
00146855 Flute · 00146863 Horn
00146858 Clarinet · 00146864 Trombone
00146859 Alto Sax · 00146866 Violin
00146860 Tenor Sax · 00146867 Viola
00146862 Trumpet · 00146868 Cello

Contemporary Broadway
15 songs
00298704 Flute · 00298709 Horn
00298705 Clarinet · 00298710 Trombone
00298706 Alto Sax · 00298711 Violin
00298707 Tenor Sax · 00298712 Viola
00298708 Trumpet · 00298713 Cello

Disney Movie Hits
12 songs
00841420 Flute · 00841424 Horn
00841687 Oboe · 00841425 Trombone
00841421 Clarinet · 00841426 Violin
00841422 Alto Sax · 00841427 Viola
00841686 Tenor Sax · 00841428 Cello
00841423 Trumpet

Prices, contents, and availability subject to change without notice.

Disney Solos
12 songs
00841404 Flute · 00841506 Oboe
00841406 Alto Sax · 00841409 Trumpet
00841407 Horn · 00841410 Violin
00841411 Viola · 00841412 Cello
00841405 Clarinet/Tenor Sax
00841408 Trombone/Baritone
00841553 Mallet Percussion

Dixieland Favorites
15 songs
00268756 Flute · 0068759 Trumpet
00268757 Clarinet · 00268760 Trombone
00268758 Alto Sax

Billie Eilish
9 songs
00345648 Flute · 00345653 Horn
00345649 Clarinet · 00345654 Trombone
00345650 Alto Sax · 00345655 Violin
00345651 Tenor Sax · 00345656 Viola
00345652 Trumpet · 00345657 Cello

Favorite Movie Themes
13 songs
00841166 Flute · 00841168 Trumpet
00841167 Clarinet · 00841170 Trombone
00841169 Alto Sax · 00841296 Violin

Gospel Hymns
15 songs
00194648 Flute · 00194654 Trombone
00194649 Clarinet · 00194655 Violin
00194650 Alto Sax · 00194656 Viola
00194651 Tenor Sax · 00194657 Cello
00194652 Trumpet

Great Classical Themes
15 songs
00292727 Flute · 00292733 Horn
00292728 Clarinet · 00292735 Trombone
00292729 Alto Sax · 00292736 Violin
00292730 Tenor Sax · 00292737 Viola
00292732 Trumpet · 00292738 Cello

The Greatest Showman
8 songs
00277389 Flute · 00277394 Horn
00277390 Clarinet · 00277395 Trombone
00277391 Alto Sax · 00277396 Violin
00277392 Tenor Sax · 00277397 Viola
00277393 Trumpet · 00277398 Cello

Irish Favorites
31 songs
00842489 Flute · 00842495 Trombone
00842490 Clarinet · 00842496 Violin
00842491 Alto Sax · 00842497 Viola
00842493 Trumpet · 00842498 Cello
00842494 Horn

Michael Jackson
11 songs
00119495 Flute · 00119499 Trumpet
00119496 Clarinet · 00119501 Trombone
00119497 Alto Sax · 00119503 Violin
00119498 Tenor Sax · 00119502 Accomp.

Jazz & Blues
14 songs
00841438 Flute · 00841441 Trumpet
00841439 Clarinet · 00841443 Trombone
00841440 Alto Sax · 00841444 Violin
00841442 Tenor Sax

Jazz Classics
12 songs
00151812 Flute · 00151816 Trumpet
00151813 Clarinet · 00151818 Trombone
00151814 Alto Sax · 00151819 Violin
00151815 Tenor Sax · 00151821 Cello

Les Misérables
13 songs
00842292 Flute · 00842297 Horn
00842293 Clarinet · 00842298 Trombone
00842294 Alto Sax · 00842299 Violin
00842295 Tenor Sax · 00842300 Viola
00842296 Trumpet · 00842301 Cello

Metallica
12 songs
02501327 Flute · 02502454 Horn
02501339 Clarinet · 02501329 Trombone
02501332 Alto Sax · 02501334 Violin
02501333 Tenor Sax · 02501335 Viola
02501330 Trumpet · 02501338 Cello

Motown Classics
15 songs
00842572 Flute · 00842576 Trumpet
00842573 Clarinet · 00842578 Trombone
00842574 Alto Sax · 00842579 Violin
00842575 Tenor Sax

Pirates of the Caribbean
16 songs
00842183 Flute · 00842188 Horn
00842184 Clarinet · 00842189 Trombone
00842185 Alto Sax · 00842190 Violin
00842186 Tenor Sax · 00842191 Viola
00842187 Trumpet · 00842192 Cello

Queen
17 songs
00285402 Flute · 00285407 Horn
00285403 Clarinet · 00285408 Trombone
00285404 Alto Sax · 00285409 Violin
00285405 Tenor Sax · 00285410 Viola
00285406 Trumpet · 00285411 Cello

Simple Songs
14 songs
00249081 Flute · 00249087 Horn
00249093 Oboe · 00249089 Trombone
00249082 Clarinet · 00249090 Violin
00249083 Alto Sax · 00249091 Viola
00249084 Tenor Sax · 00249092 Cello
00249086 Trumpet · 00249094 Mallets

Superhero Themes
14 songs
00363195 Flute · 00363200 Horn
00363196 Clarinet · 00363201 Trombone
00363197 Alto Sax · 00363202 Violin
00363198 Tenor Sax · 00363203 Viola
00363199 Trumpet · 00363204 Cello

Star Wars
16 songs
00350900 Flute · 00350907 Horn
00350913 Oboe · 00350908 Trombone
00350903 Clarinet · 00350909 Violin
00350904 Alto Sax · 00350910 Viola
00350905 Tenor Sax · 00350911 Cello
00350906 Trumpet · 00350914 Mallet

Taylor Swift
15 songs
00842532 Flute · 00842537 Horn
00842533 Clarinet · 00842538 Trombone
00842534 Alto Sax · 00842539 Violin
00842535 Tenor Sax · 00842540 Viola
00842536 Trumpet · 00842541 Cello

Video Game Music
13 songs
00283877 Flute · 00283883 Horn
00283878 Clarinet · 00283884 Trombone
00283879 Alto Sax · 00283885 Violin
00283880 Tenor Sax · 00283886 Viola
00283882 Trumpet · 00283887 Cello

Wicked
13 songs
00842236 Flute · 00842241 Horn
00842237 Clarinet · 00842242 Trombone
00842238 Alto Sax · 00842243 Violin
00842239 Tenor Sax · 00842244 Viola
00842240 Trumpet · 00842245 Cello

HAL•LEONARD®

0122
488

THE ULTIMATE COLLECTION OF
FAKE BOOKS

The Real Book – Sixth Edition

Hal Leonard proudly presents the first legitimate and legal editions of these books ever produced. These bestselling titles are mandatory for anyone who plays jazz! Over 400 songs, including: All By Myself • Dream a Little Dream of Me • God Bless the Child • Like Someone in Love • When I Fall in Love • and more.

00240221 Volume 1, C Instruments $45.00
00240224 Volume 1, B♭ Instruments $45.00
00240225 Volume 1, E♭ Instruments $45.00
00240226 Volume 1, BC Instruments $45.00

Go to halleonard.com to view all *Real Books* available

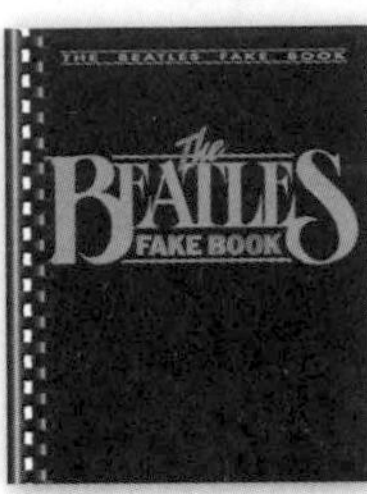

The Beatles Fake Book

200 of the Beatles' hits: All You Need Is Love • Blackbird • Can't Buy Me Love • Day Tripper • Eleanor Rigby • The Fool on the Hill • Hey Jude • In My Life • Let It Be • Michelle • Norwegian Wood (This Bird Has Flown) • Penny Lane • Revolution • She Loves You • Twist and Shout • With a Little Help from My Friends • Yesterday • and many more!

00240069 C Instruments $39.99

The Best Fake Book Ever

More than 1,000 songs from all styles of music: All My Loving • At the Hop • Cabaret • Dust in the Wind • Fever • Hello, Dolly • Hey Jude • King of the Road • Longer • Misty • Route 66 • Sentimental Journey • Somebody • Song Sung Blue • Spinning Wheel • Unchained Melody • We Will Rock You • What a Wonderful World • Wooly Bully • Y.M.C.A. • and more.

00290239 C Instruments $49.99
00240084 E♭ Instruments $49.95

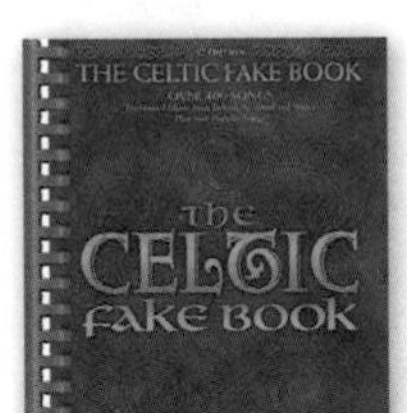

The Celtic Fake Book

Over 400 songs from Ireland, Scotland and Wales: Auld Lang Syne • Barbara Allen • Danny Boy • Finnegan's Wake • The Galway Piper • Irish Rover • Loch Lomond • Molly Malone • My Bonnie Lies Over the Ocean • My Wild Irish Rose • That's an Irish Lullaby • and more. Includes Gaelic lyrics where applicable and a pronunciation guide.

00240153 C Instruments $25.00

Classic Rock Fake Book

Over 250 of the best rock songs of all time: American Woman • Beast of Burden • Carry On Wayward Son • Dream On • Free Ride • Hurts So Good • I Shot the Sheriff • Layla • My Generation • Nights in White Satin • Owner of a Lonely Heart • Rhiannon • Roxanne • Summer of '69 • We Will Rock You • You Ain't Seen Nothin' Yet • and lots more!

00240108 C Instruments $35.00

Classical Fake Book

This unprecedented, amazingly comprehensive reference includes over 850 classical themes and melodies for all classical music lovers. Includes everything from Renaissance music to Vivaldi and Mozart to Mendelssohn. Lyrics in the original language are included when appropriate.

00240044 .... $39.99

The Disney Fake Book

Even more Disney favorites, including: The Bare Necessities • Can You Feel the Love Tonight • Circle of Life • How Do You Know? • Let It Go • Part of Your World • Reflection • Some Day My Prince Will Come • When I See an Elephant Fly • You'll Be in My Heart • and many more.

00175311 C Instruments $34.99

Disney characters & artwork TM & © 2021 Disney

The Folksong Fake Book

Over 1,000 folksongs: Bury Me Not on the Lone Prairie • Clementine • The Erie Canal • Go, Tell It on the Mountain • Home on the Range • Kumbaya • Michael Row the Boat Ashore • Shenandoah • Simple Gifts • Swing Low, Sweet Chariot • When Johnny Comes Marching Home • Yankee Doodle • and many more.

00240151 .... $34.99

The Hal Leonard Real Jazz Standards Fake Book

Over 250 standards in easy-to-read authentic hand-written jazz engravings: Ain't Misbehavin' • Blue Skies • Crazy He Calls Me • Desafinado (Off Key) • Fever • How High the Moon • It Don't Mean a Thing (If It Ain't Got That Swing) • Lazy River • Mood Indigo • Old Devil Moon • Route 66 • Satin Doll • Witchcraft • and more.

00240161 C Instruments $45.00

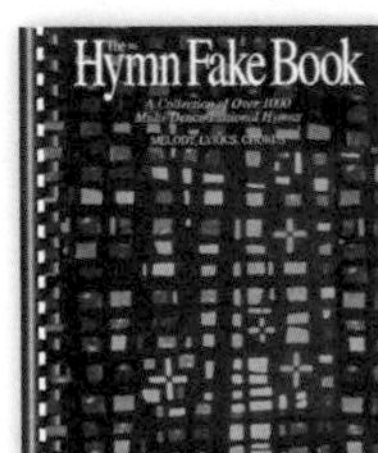

The Hymn Fake Book

Nearly 1,000 multi-denominational hymns perfect for church musicians or hobbyists: Amazing Grace • Christ the Lord Is Risen Today • For the Beauty of the Earth • It Is Well with My Soul • A Mighty Fortress Is Our God • O for a Thousand Tongues to Sing • Praise to the Lord, the Almighty • Take My Life and Let It Be • What a Friend We Have in Jesus • and hundreds more!

00240145 C Instruments $29.99

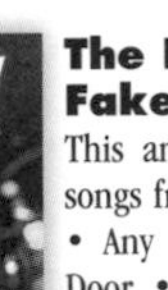

The New Broadway Fake Book

This amazing collection includes 645 songs from 285 shows: All I Ask of You • Any Dream Will Do • Close Every Door • Consider Yourself • Dancing Queen • Mack the Knife • Mamma Mia • Memory • The Phantom of the Opera • Popular • Strike up the Band • and more!

00138905 C Instruments $45.00

The Praise & Worship Fake Book

Over 400 songs including: Amazing Grace (My Chains Are Gone) • Cornerstone • Everlasting God • Great Are You Lord • In Christ Alone • Mighty to Save • Open the Eyes of My Heart • Shine, Jesus, Shine • This Is Amazing Grace • and more.

00160838 C Instruments $39.99
00240324 B♭ Instruments $34.99

Three Chord Songs Fake Book

200 classic and contemporary 3-chord tunes in melody/lyric/chord format: Ain't No Sunshine • Bang a Gong (Get It On) • Cold, Cold Heart • Don't Worry, Be Happy • Give Me One Reason • I Got You (I Feel Good) • Kiss • Me and Bobby McGee • Rock This Town • Werewolves of London • You Don't Mess Around with Jim • and more.

00240387 .... $34.99

The Ultimate Christmas Fake Book

The 6th edition of this bestseller features over 270 traditional and contemporary Christmas hits: Have Yourself a Merry Little Christmas • I'll Be Home for Christmas O Come, All Ye Faithful (Adeste Fideles) • Santa Baby • Winter Wonderland • and more.

00147215 C Instruments $30.00

The Ultimate Country Fake Book

This book includes over 700 of your favorite country hits: Always on My Mind • Boot Scootin' Boogie • Crazy • Down at the Twist and Shout • Forever and Ever, Amen • Friends in Low Places • The Gambler • Jambalaya • King of the Road • Sixteen Tons • There's a Tear in My Beer • Your Cheatin' Heart • and hundreds more.

00240049 C Instruments $49.99

The Ultimate Fake Book

Includes over 1,200 hits: Blue Skies • Body and Soul • Endless Love • Isn't It Romantic? • Memory • Mona Lisa • Moon River • Operator • Piano Man • Roxanne • Satin Doll • Shout • Small World • Smile • Speak Softly, Love • Strawberry Fields Forever • Tears in Heaven • Unforgettable • hundreds more!

00240024 C Instruments $55.00
00240026 B♭ Instruments $49.95

The Ultimate Jazz Fake Book

This must-own collection includes 635 songs spanning all jazz styles from more than 9 decades. Songs include: Maple Leaf Rag • Basin Street Blues • A Night in Tunisia • Lullaby of Birdland • The Girl from Ipanema • Bag's Groove • I Can't Get Started • All the Things You Are • and many more!

00240079 C Instruments $45.00
00240080 B♭ Instruments $45.00
00240081 E♭ Instruments $45.00

The Ultimate Rock Pop Fake Book

This amazing collection features nearly 550 rock and pop hits: American Pie • Bohemian Rhapsody • Born to Be Wild • Clocks • Dancing with Myself • Eye of the Tiger • Proud Mary • Rocket Man • Should I Stay or Should I Go • Total Eclipse of the Heart • Unchained Melody • When Doves Cry • Y.M.C.A. • You Raise Me Up • and more.

00240310 C Instruments $39.99

Complete songlists available online at **www.halleonard.com**